Know Your Numbers

Ants at the Picnic

Counting by Tens

by Michael Dahl

illustrated by Zachary Trover

Special thanks to our advisers for their expertise:

Stuart Farm, M.Ed., Mathematics Lecturer
University of North Dakota, Grand Forks

Susan Kesselring, M.A., Literacy Educator
Rosemount–Apple Valley–Eagan (Minnesota) School District

PICTURE WINDOW BOOKS
Minneapolis, Minnesota

MUSTARD

Editor: Christianne Jones
Designer: Jaime Martens
Page Production: Zachary Trover
Creative Director: Keith Griffin
Editorial Director: Carol Jones
The illustrations in this book were created digitally.

Picture Window Books
5115 Excelsior Boulevard
Suite 232
Minneapolis, MN 55416
877-845-8392
www.picturewindowbooks.com

Printed in the United States of America.

Library of Congress Cataloging-in-Publication Data
Dahl, Michael.
Ants at the picnic : counting by tens / by Michael Dahl ;
illustrated by Zachary Trover.
p. cm. — (Know your numbers)
Includes bibliographical references and index.
ISBN 1-4048-1318-7 (hardcover)
1. Counting—Juvenile literature. 2. Addition—Juvenile
literature. 3. Ants—Juvenile literature. 4. Picnicking—
Juvenile literature. I. Trover, Zachary, ill. II. Title.
QA113.D324 2006
513.2'11—dc22   2005021816

It's picnic time,
what a perfect spot!
Grass and shade,
it's not too hot.

Coolers, blankets, and tunes for a dance.
Lots of food, and LOTS OF ANTS!

ONE HUNDRED ants at the picnic.

No potato salad today.
The salad bowl just marched away.

10 20 30 40 50 60 70 80 90 100

NINETY ants at the picnic.

6

The pickles are gone,
    just as I feared.

10 20 30 40 50 60 70 80 90

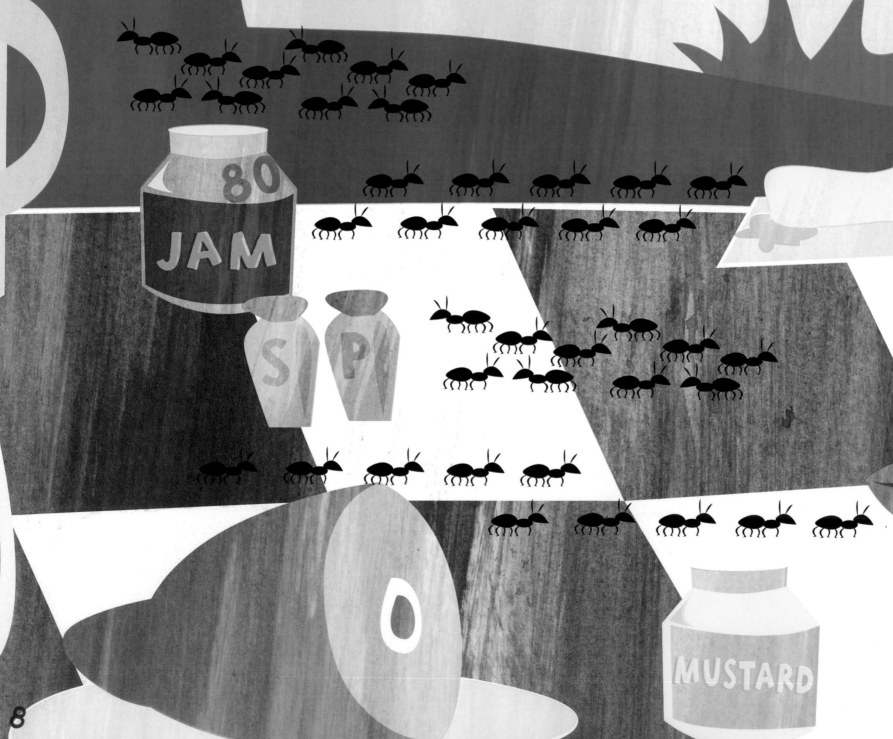

EIGHTY ants at the picnic.

8

The hot dog buns have disappeared!

SEVENTY ants at the picnic.

I can't find the serving spoon!

SIXTY ants at the picnic.

The chocolate cake has gone too soon!

60

| 10 | 20 | 30 | 40 | 50 | 60 |

FIFTY ants at the picnic.

14

FORTY ants at the picnic.

No more butter! No more jam!

THIRTY ants at the picnic.

S P

Has anyone seen the watermelon?

30

10 20 30

19

TWENTY ants at the picnic.

TEN ants at the picnic.
Nothing to eat, and nothing to drink.

But all the ants are gone I think!

10

10

23

Fun Facts

 Ants can lift and carry more than 50 times their own weight.

 Ants cannot chew their food. Instead, they move their jaws like scissors to get the juices out of the food.

 Ants stretch when they wake up. They also appear to yawn like humans.

 Ants live in colonies. They may have as many as 500,000 ants in one colony.

 Ants don't have eyelids. Their eyes are always open, even when they're sleeping.

On the Web

FactHound offers a safe, fun way to find Internet sites related to this book. All of the sites on FactHound have been researched by our staff.

1. Visit www.facthound.com

2. Type in this special code for age-appropriate sites: 1404813187

3. Click on the FETCH IT button.

Your trusty FactHound will fetch the best sites for you!

Find the Numbers

Now you have finished reading the story, but a surprise still awaits you. Hidden in each picture is a multiple of ten from 10 to 100. Can you find them all?

10–in the lemonade
20–on Aunt Helen's shoulder
30–on the watermelon
40–on the watermelon
50–on the ham
60–on the cake
70–on the ham
80–on the jam jar
90–on the picnic blanket
100–on the pickel

Look for all of the books in the Know Your Numbers series: